P9-EEM-891

Hey! You're Reading in the Wrong Direction!

This is the ***end*** of this graphic novel!

To properly enjoy this VIZ graphic novel, please turn it around and begin reading from ***right to left.*** Unlike English, Japanese is read right to left, so Japanese comics are read in reverse order from the way English comics are typically read.

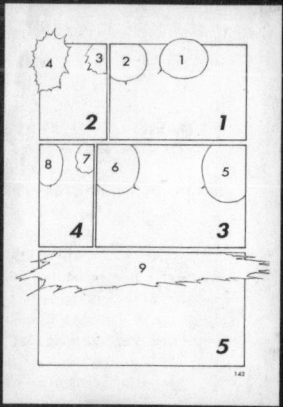

Follow the action this way

This book has been printed in the original Japanese format in order to preserve the orientation of the original artwork. Have fun with it!

Hillsboro Public Library
Hillsboro, OR
A member of Washington County
COOPERATIVE LIBRARY SERVICES
WITHDRAWN

THE LEGEND OF ZELDA™

Twilight Princess

Volume 10—VIZ Media Edition

STORY AND ART BY
Akira Himekawa

DRAWING STAFF Akiko Mori / Sakiho Tsutsui / Kanan

TRANSLATION John Werry
ENGLISH ADAPTATION Stan!
TOUCH-UP ART & LETTERING Evan Waldinger
DESIGNER Shawn Carrico
EDITOR Mike Montesa

33614082999995

THE LEGEND OF ZELDA: TWILIGHT PRINCESS
TM & © 2022 Nintendo. All Rights Reserved.

ZELDA NO DENSETSU TWILIGHT PRINCESS Vol. 10
by Akira HIMEKAWA
© 2016 Akira HIMEKAWA
All rights reserved.
Original Japanese edition published by SHOGAKUKAN.
English translation rights in the United States of America, Canada, the United Kingdom, Ireland, Australia and New Zealand arranged with SHOGAKUKAN.

Original design by Kazutada YOKOYAMA

The stories, characters, and incidents mentioned in this publication are entirely fictional.

No portion of this book may be reproduced or transmitted in any form or by any means without written permission from the copyright holders.

Printed in the U.S.A.

Published by VIZ Media, LLC
P.O. Box 77010
San Francisco, CA 94107

10 9 8 7 6 5 4 3 2 1
First printing, September 2022

AUTHOR'S NOTE

The final boss in *The Legend of Zelda* is always Ganondorf (Ganon), but Link in *Twilight Princess* is confronting him for the first time. Why must they fight? What does he believe in?

He has finally arrived at this place.

Akira Himekawa is the collaboration of two women, A. Honda and S. Nagano. Together they have created ten manga adventures featuring Link and the popular video game world of *The Legend of Zelda*™. Their most recent work, *The Legend of Zelda*™*: Twilight Princess*, is serialized digitally on Shogakukan's MangaONE app in Japan.

ZRRIP

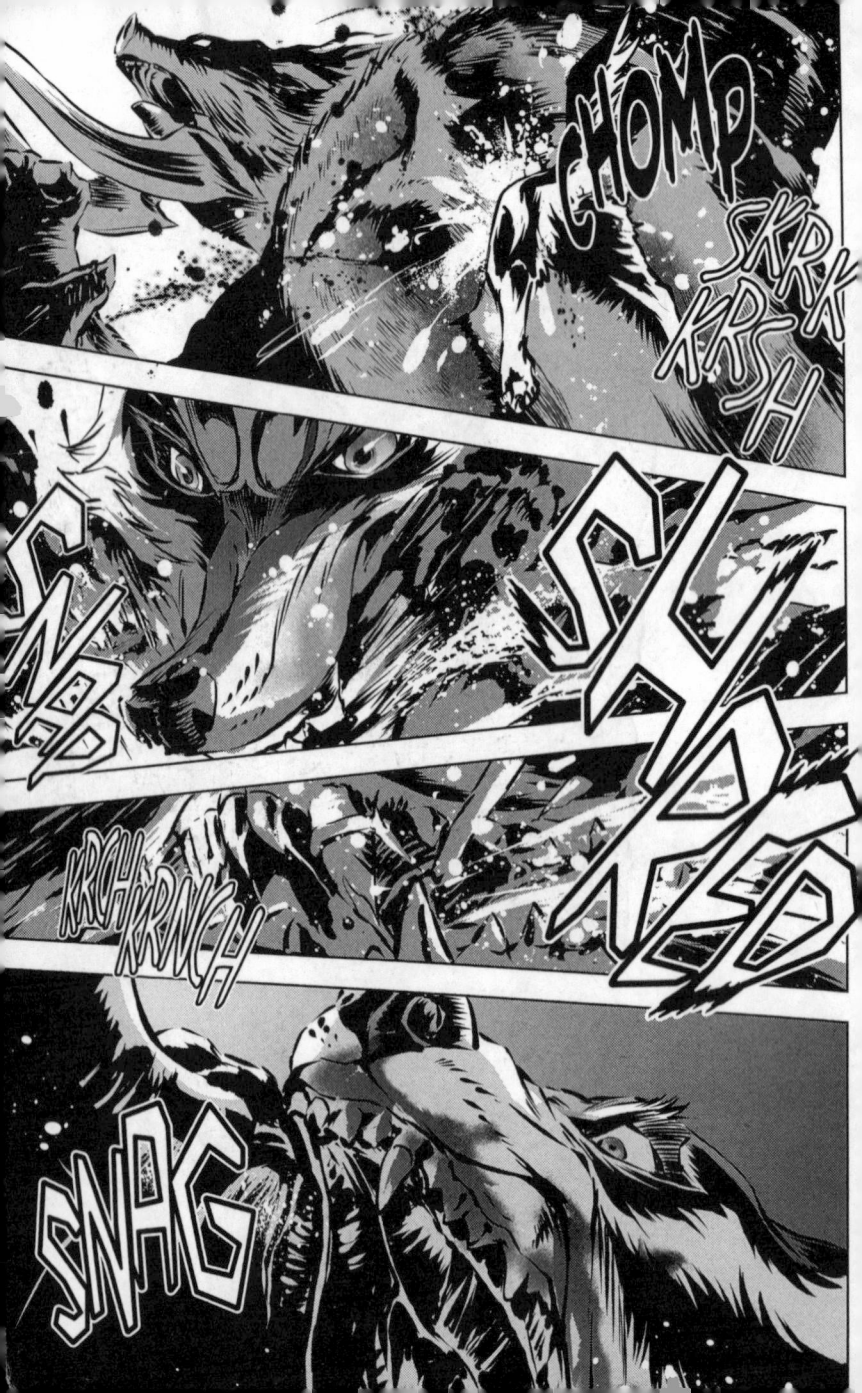
CHOMP
SKRK
KRSH
SKRED
KRCH
KRNCH
SNAG

CHOMP
GRRR
GNASH
GNAW
GLAGH
RRIP

GRRR
WHOA!
AH
GWUP

YONK
SWSSH
I'LL HOLD HIM IN PLACE!
CALM DOWN...
...YOU SELFISH OLD MAN!

LINK?!
THOMM
KRAKKKK
THW
MP
AWE-SOME!
GRRRRRR

GRRRAH
KRASH

GRRR

AWOOO

GRRRRRRR
FWSH
IF HATE TURNS YOU INTO A BEAST...
...THEN ANGER TURNS ME INTO ONE!
WITH MY FANGS OF ANGER...
...I WILL SHRED YOUR UNDYING HATE AND GREED!

DO NOT INTERFERE WITH ME ANY LONGER!
LINK ?!
FWSH
SWSH
MY TRIFORCE ISN'T THE SLIGHTEST BIT INTIMIDATED BY YOUR HATE!
I SAY THE SAME TO YOU!

...THAT FEEL LIKE THEY'RE STABBING MY SKIN.
THE FLAMES OF HATRED RADIATE WAVES OF PAIN...
...THAT MUCH?
DOES HE REALLY HATE ME...

IS THE TRIFORCE OF POWER RAGING OUT OF CONTROL?
OR IS THAT DARK BEAST THE VERY INCARNATION OF GREED?
GRRR
ARR
ROOO

W...
WHAT IS THAT?!
IS THAT GANON-DORF?!
GRRR

THAT... IMMENSE POWER...!
MINE ...
TRIFORCE ...!
GROOOHH
IT'S ALL MINE!

ZWAAAA
A
A
A
A
HEEF
HEEF
HEEF
CHK
DWK
HEEF
HZZZ
HEEF
A
A
A
HZZZ
TRI
...
...
FORCE!

SHF SHF
YOUR HAIR'S BURNT!
YOU'VE BEEN THROUGH A LOT.
GUESS THE HERO COULDN'T HURT THE PRINCESS. I THOUGHT AS MUCH!
MIDNA! ARE YOU ALL RIGHT?
WOOO
WOOOO

P-PRINCESS ZELDA...!
THAT WAS CLOSE, HUH?
...M-M...

HHHH
HHHH
GYAAAGH!
ZELDA...
...HAVE SUCH SAD EYES.
...YOU MUST NO LONGER...

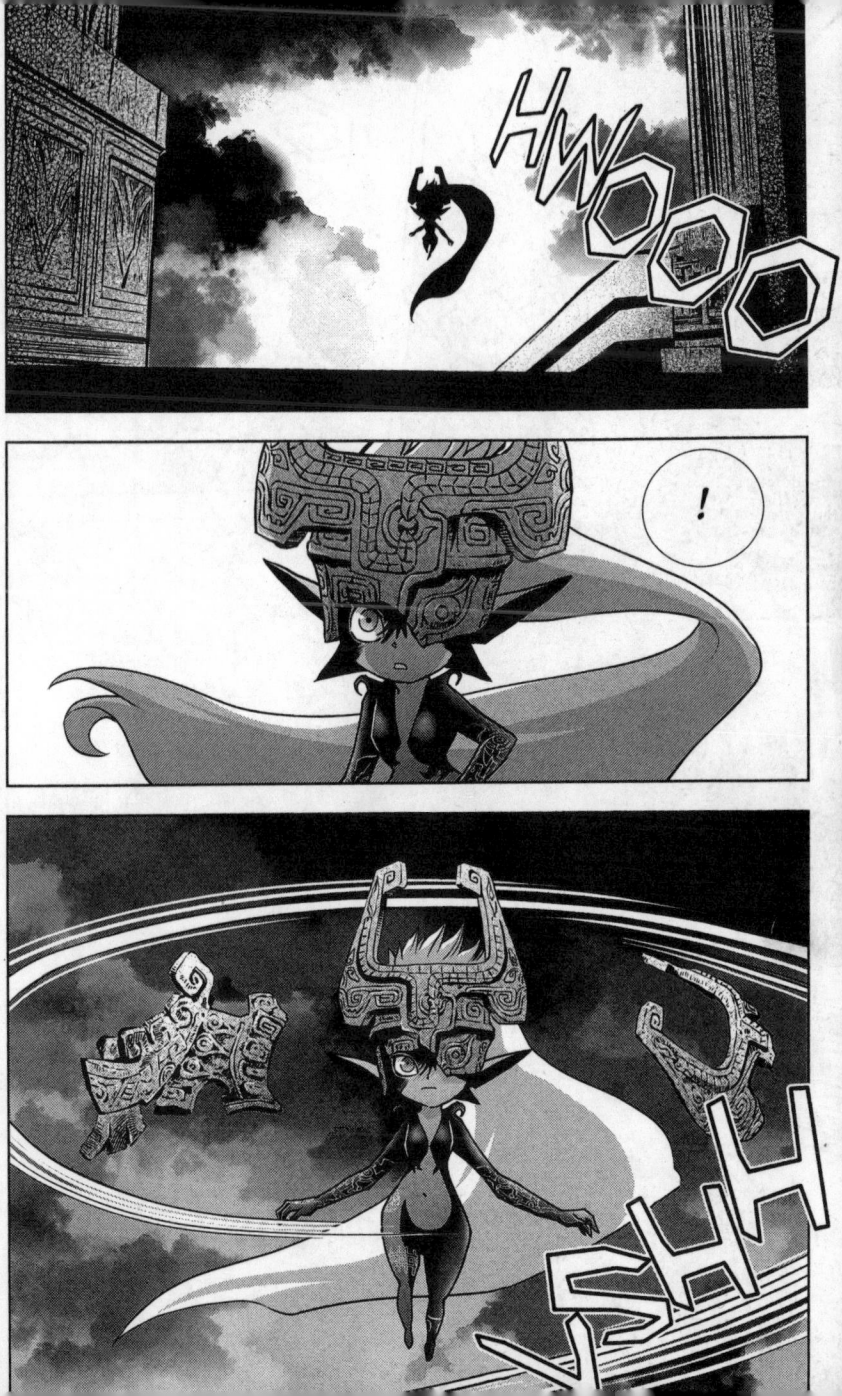
HWOOO
!
SHH

GRAB
SHING
ZELDA!
NOOOO!

GRIP
SHNNNN
?!
...
W...
WHAT ARE YOU DOING?
SHWP

NOW...
... SHALL I SKEWER YOU A TIME OR TWO?
IN THE EYE?
BUT WHERE ...?
THE THROAT?
BOOT
SHING
I CAN'T HARM PRINCESS ZELDA.
IT'S NO USE...
I CAN'T DO IT, NO MATTER WHAT!
FIRST, I'LL PRICK OUT THAT IMPUDENT ...
... EYE!

... WILL NOT BE SATISFIED BY MERELY KILLING YOU ONCE OR TWICE.
... AND RELISH YOUR LINGERING CRIES OF PAIN.
I MUST CRUSH YOUR BONES ...
... RIP OUT YOUR ORGANS ...

IT IS NOT NEARLY ENOUGH TO BALANCE OUT...
... MY HATRED FOR YOU!
...
HATRED?
IF IT WEREN'T FOR YOU...
... I WOULD HAVE ALREADY ESTABLISHED MY REIGN.
I WOULD HAVE WHAT I DESIRED.
MY HATRED TOWARD YOU, THE ONE WHO TOOK EVERYTHING FROM ME...

WHAK
GAAH!
YOU LOOK WRETCHED.
BUT THIS ISN'T ENOUGH.
WHMP

A-ARE YOU...
...YOUR LIFE FORCE?
... G-GIVING ME...

BAKOOM

"I DON'T UNDERSTAND, AURU."
"WHY DO YOU HATE THE TWILIGHT REALM SO MUCH?"
SKCH
SKCH
LINK ...!
"...YOU'RE JUST LOOKING FOR AN EVIL YOU CAN SAFELY OPPOSE."
"TO HIDE YOUR OWN WEAKNESS AND SHAME..."
FOR MY HOMELAND!
WAS...
WAS THAT SO WRONG?!
...OF THE ROYAL FAMILY...
AS A SERVANT...
BUT ONLY TO KEEP THE SHADOW AWAY AND PROTECT HYRULE!
...I TURNED MYSELF INTO A DEMON!

MIDNA!
THUMP
THUMP
THUMP
OOOF!
KLANG
SKCH
SKCH
SKCH
LINK ...!
I HAVE TO HELP LINK...!

LINK ...!
LINK IS IN DANGER!
IF I'M NOT THERE ...!
LINK WILL BE FINE! HE'S GOING TO DEFEAT THE DEMON KING!
SLASH
HE DOESN'T MIND IF HE DOES.
HE INTENDS TO GIVE HIS LIFE TO FIGHT THE DEMON KING.
?!
LINK IS PLANNING TO DIE.

LET ME HAVE SOME MORE FUN.
KEEEE
AGH!
LLLT
... THAT YOU VALUE SO HIGHLY!
SHOW ME THE LOYALTY, FRIENDSHIP, AND SELF-SACRIFICE...
KZZZT

P-PRINCESS ZELDA!!
SHING
CAN'T YOU DO ANYTHING ANYMORE?
WHERE'S ALL THAT SPIRIT YOU HAD BEFORE?

ドン
AAHEEE!
KIIKIIKII
BIII
GRK

WHAT CAN I DO TO BREAK GANONDORF'S SPELL...
...OVER PRINCESS ZELDA?!
#52. THE LORD'S HALL, PART 3
BZZT
BZZT BZZT
BZZT
KOOM
BWOK

FW
SH
HA HA HA
HA HA
NOW FIGHT!
IF YOU DON'T BEAT ME, YOU CAN'T DEFEAT THE DEMON KING.
ZUD

GET OUT OF PRINCESS ZELDA'S BODY RIGHT NOW!
HEH HEH HEH ...
THIS IS WHAT THE PRINCESS HERSELF WANTED!
WHAT ?!
PRINCESS ZELDA HAS JOINED THE DEMON KING.
WE TALKED IT OVER, AND WHEN I PROPOSED RULING THE WORLD TOGETHER, SHE GLADLY AGREED.
DON'T BEFOUL PRINCESS ZELDA'S HONOR WITH SUCH LIES!
THE MOST NOBLE GANDONDORF...
... IS THE RIGHTFUL RULER OF THIS WORLD.

FOOL WHO REBELS AGAINST THE KING WHO WOULD RULE LIGHT AND SHADOW...
... GROVEL BEFORE THE GREAT DEMON KING...
... AND HAND OVER THE TRIFORCE OF COURAGE.

FWSH

SLUMP
YAAAAH!!
WHAT DID YOU DO?!
GANON-DORF ...
PRINCESS-
PRINCES ZELDA?!

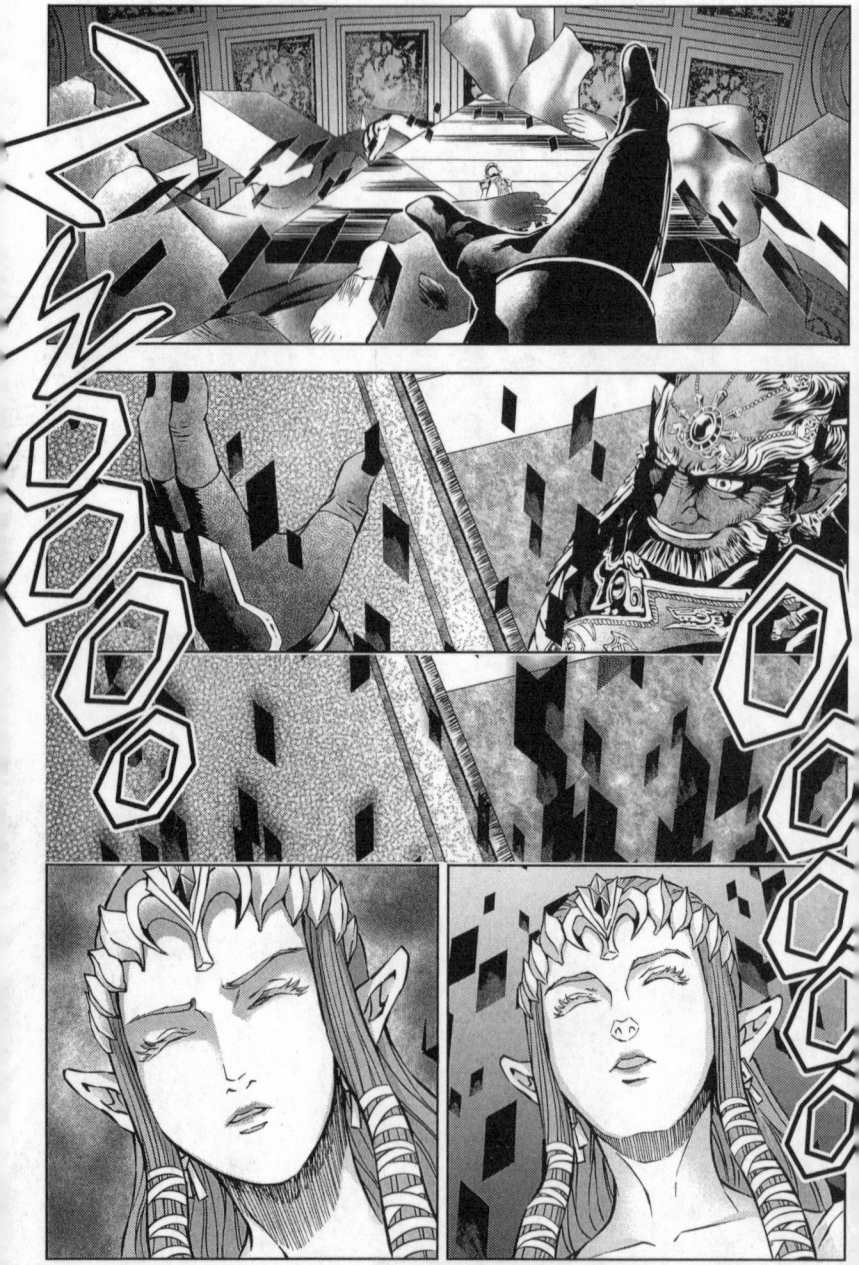

EVEN IF THE GODS WISH IT...
...I WON'T PERMIT IT!
TRY STOPPING ME, YOUNG ONE.

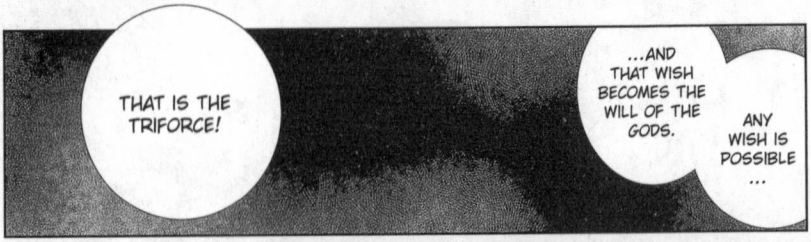
THAT IS THE TRIFORCE!
...AND THAT WISH BECOMES THE WILL OF THE GODS.
ANY WISH IS POSSIBLE ...

IT IS THE WILL OF THE GODS THAT I BECOME RULER!

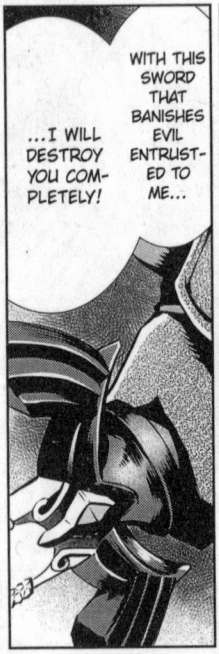
WITH THIS SWORD THAT BANISHES EVIL ENTRUSTED TO ME...
...I WILL DESTROY YOU COMPLETELY!

I WON'T LET YOU TRAMPLE THE LAND OF HYRULE AGAIN!
THAT DREAM WILL NEVER COME TRUE, NOT FOR ALL ETERNITY.
THE SAME GOES FOR THE TWILIGHT REALM.

RETURN THE TRIFORCE OF POWER!
DO IT NOW.
THAT IS YOUR ONLY ROAD TO SALVATION.
IF THE TRIFORCE TRULY IS THE POWER OF THE GODS...
...
...WE SHOULD GIVE IT BACK IT TO THEM.
YOU'RE THE FIRST PERSON TO EVER SAY THAT TO ME.
HA HA HA
HOW HUMOR-OUS!
"YOUR WISH IS NOW OUR WISH TOO."
IT GRANTS THE FIRST WISH OF WHOEVER TOUCHES IT.
THE TRIFORCE IS A GOLDEN RELIC THAT THE GODS LEFT ON THE SURFACE OF THE WORLD AT THE TIME OF ITS CREATION.

THE ONE WHO CONTROLS THAT POWER...
...IS THE ONLY ONE FIT TO RULE THIS WORLD!
WHEN THE THREE TRIFORCES ARE IN MY HANDS, MY DREAMS WILL BE REALIZED.
THE TIME I HAVE SO DESPERATELY DESIRED IS FINALLY HERE.

LONG AGO, WITH BUT LITTLE POWER, THEY CROSSED THE GODS AND WERE FORSAKEN.
THE PEOPLE OF THE TWILIGHT REALM ARE PITIFUL.

...AND THEIR HATRED BECAME STRENGTH, THUS AWAKENING ME.
THAT ANGUISH BECAME SUSTE-NANCE FOR FLESH AND BLOOD...

IT WAS *STRENGTH!*

WHAT DID THE TWILI LACK?

POWER POSSESSED ONLY BY THOSE WHOM THE GODS HAVE CHOSEN.

FINALLY ALL THREE HOLY TRIFORCES COME TOGETHER AT ONCE.
AGES HAVE PASSED SINCE THEY THWARTED MY DREAMS AND CONSIDERED ME AS GOOD AS DEAD.

YES...
...I AM GANONDORF.
I'VE BEEN WAITING FOR YOU, BOY.

AT LONG LAST, THE PLAYERS ARE ALL ONSTAGE.

SO...
...YOU'RE GANONDORF, EH?

PRINCESS ZELDA!
!!

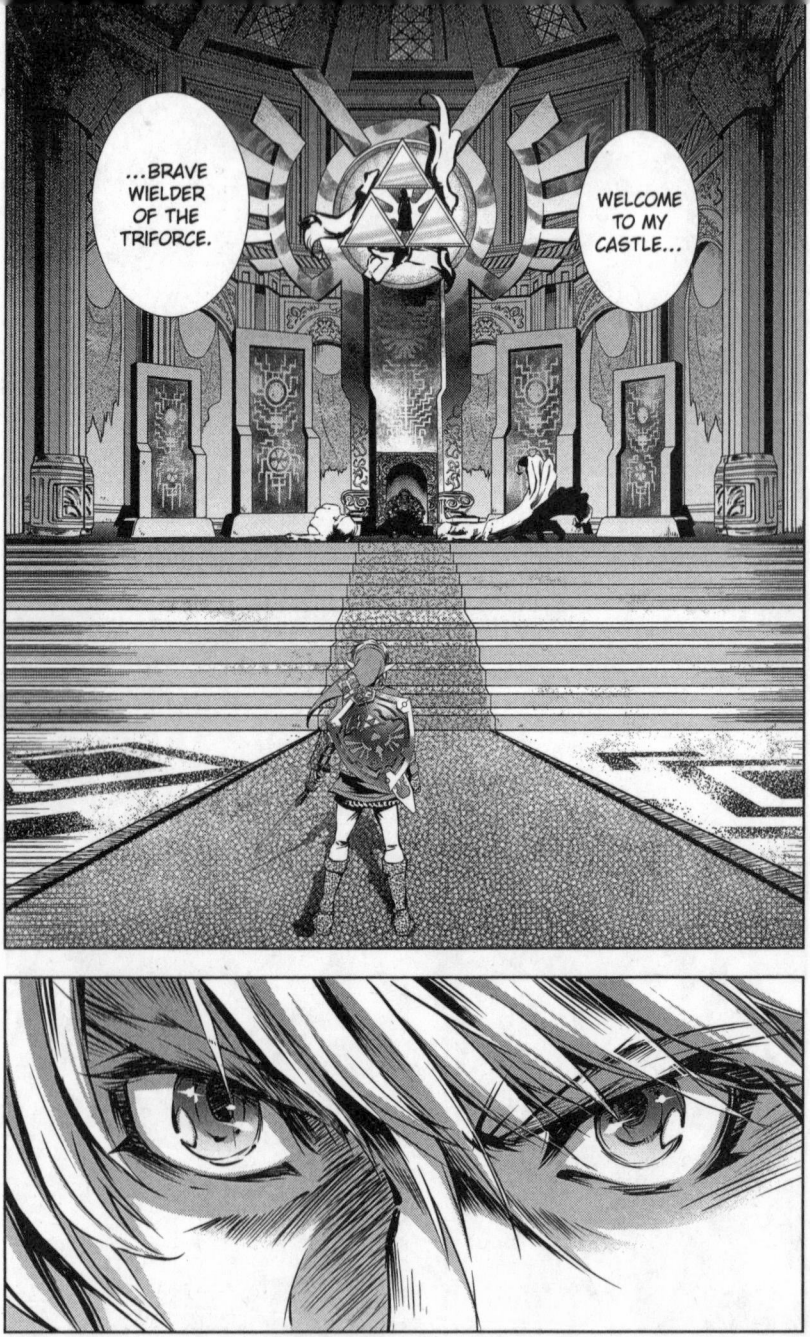
...BRAVE WIELDER OF THE TRIFORCE.
WELCOME TO MY CASTLE...

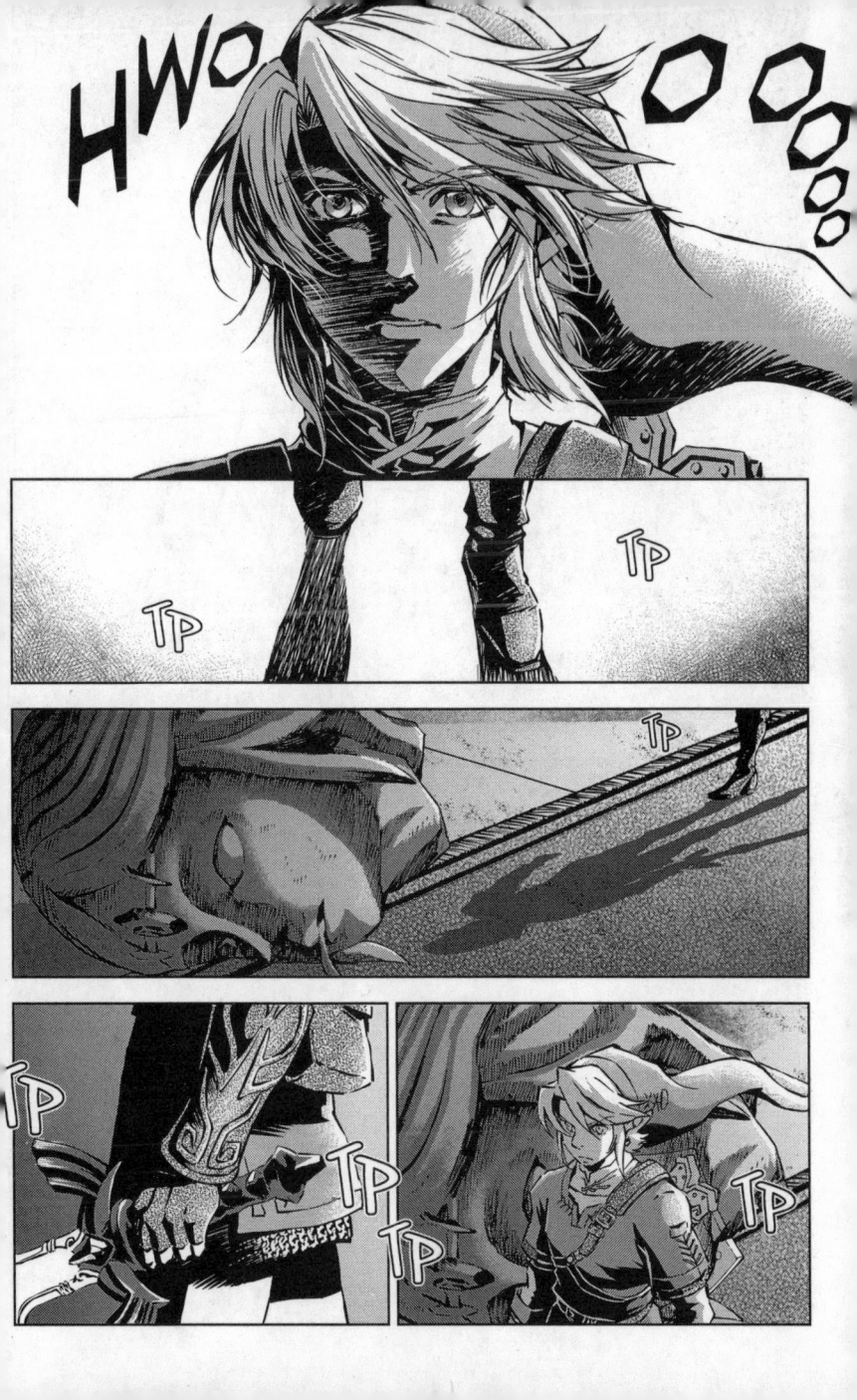
HWO
TP
TP
TP
TP
TP
TP
TP

FWOOO
RMMMBL

BECAUSE THAT'S CERTAINLY YOUR ROLE!
DARPA...
...RISE TO BECOME CAPTAIN OF THE KNIGHTS AND DEFEND HYRULE.
...SUPPORT DARPA.
ZEU...
RIOMA...
AS FOR ME...

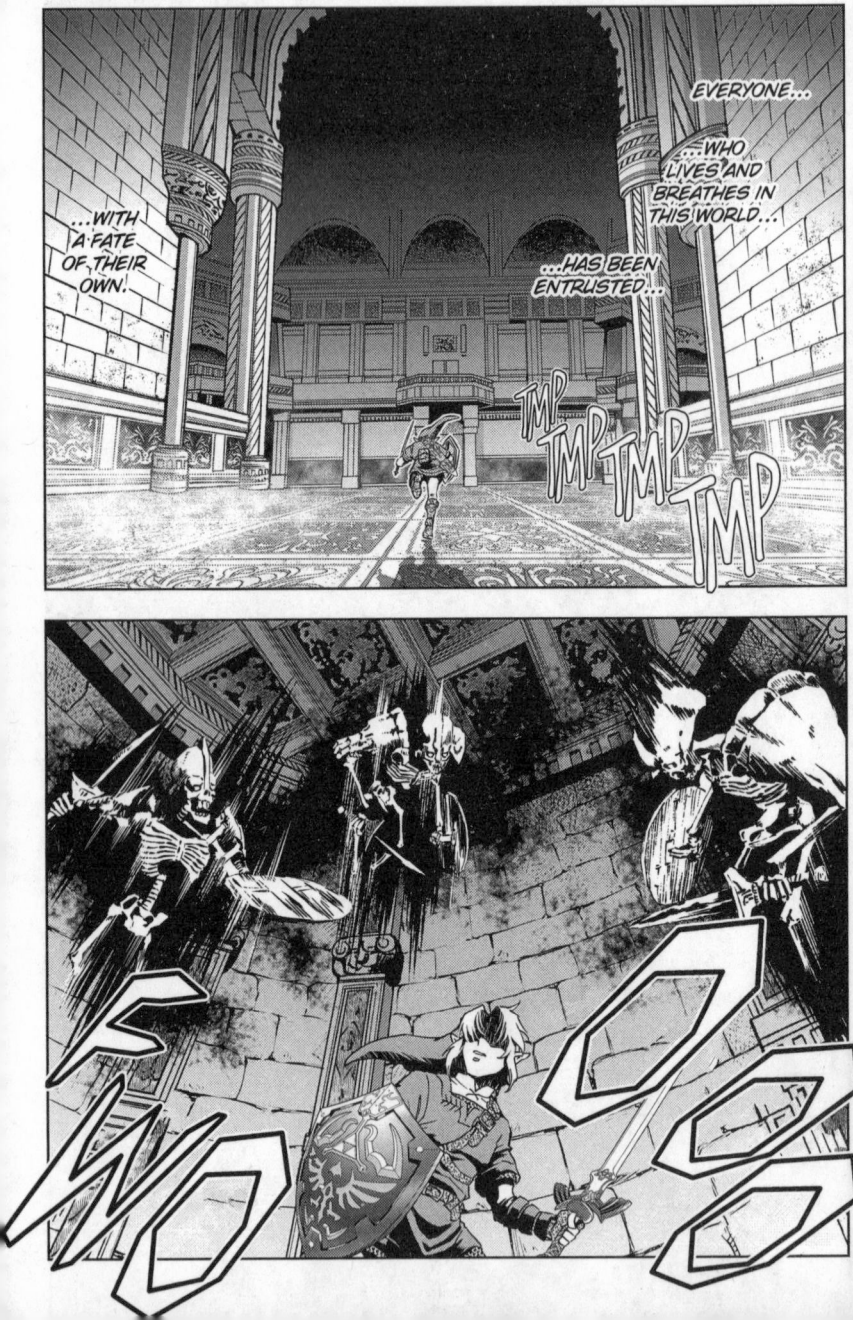
EVERYONE...
...WHO LIVES AND BREATHES IN THIS WORLD...
...HAS BEEN ENTRUSTED...
...WITH A FATE OF THEIR OWN.
TMP TMP TMP TMP

...BUT THERE'S NO DENYING HE HAD...

...HIS OWN ROLE TO PLAY.

HE WAS THE CAUSE OF SO MUCH CALAMITY.

HE PLAGUED ME FOR SO LONG...

TELL ME TO DIE AND I'LL DO IT.
YOU'RE MY MASTER NOW. GIVE ME ANY ORDER.

OKAY THEN...
I ORDER YOU...
...TO HELP MY FRIENDS FIGHTING AT THE CASTLE GATE.

HYAH!

THAT'S EASY.

YOU...!
YOU BEAT ME...
GRW
...AND I FOLLOW THE STRONG.
END OF STORY.

FWP
KTNK
KTNK
KTNK
THWAM

...THE HERO! LINK!
A LITTLE EARLIER...

I'M HELPING YOU ON MASTER'S ORDERS.
DON'T BE AFRAID.
SKF
SPLAT
YOU TRAITOR!
HUH ...?
WHO DO YOU THINK YOU'RE TALKING TO?
I SERVE ...

THOK
WHAT ARE YOU DOING ?!
K-KING BULBLIN ?!
WHAM
GLARE

WHA-BAM
KA-WHH

DO OM
GRRR

GROO
TMP
TMP
KRAK

THMP
HANG IN THERE, RIOMA!
URGH ...
THIS IS BAD...

AAA
SPLUK

HANG IN THERE, RIOMA!
THIS IS BAD...
SLRPCH!
SKKK!
URGH...

YOU'RE NOT A GREAT WARRIOR, RIGHT?
YOU SAID IT YOURSELF...
KING
RIOMA!
BUT WHAT IF I'M NOT USEFUL NOW?!
GN
NK
SO WHY AM I EVEN HERE?!
...NO MATTER HOW HARD I TRAIN.
I DON'T HAVE LINK'S OR DARPA'S TALENT WITH THE SWORD...
SHNNG
RAAAGH !!
I NEED TO BE A SHIELD DEFENDING HYRULE!
...A SINGLE MOMENT!
GRK
GRK
SKF
SOMETIMES A WHOLE BATTLE CAN HANG ON...
JUST A MOMENT IS ENOUGH!
KRX

THUD
WATCH OUT, ZEU!
THNK

WE'RE CLEARING THE WAY FOR LINK!
I DON'T CARE HOW MANY OF YOU THERE ARE!
CHOK
CHARGE!
YAAH!

#51. THE LORD'S HALL, PART 2
GRAAA
R

WHY DON'T YOU...
...TRY DANCING WITH ME!

SO...
...WE MEET AGAIN.
GRIN

!

BWAHAHAHAHA
KTNK
GUK

WHNK

ZWSHH
SHWOO

TOWOW
SWSH
SWSH
KRASH

SHASH
ZSH
!!
KLANK
KLANK

HWO

RRMM

LINK!!
SO I CAN'T LET HER DIE!
MIDNA HAS TO RULE THE TWILIGHT REALM WHEN THIS IS DONE.
AS FOR THE WORLD OF LIGHT...
I ENTRUST HYRULE TO YOU...
...MY FRIENDS!
FIGHT LIKE HELL!
DRAW AS MANY OF THE ENEMY HERE AS POSSIBLE!

WE PROMISE TO PROTECT HER.
GIVE HER HERE!

N-NO...
...LINK!
DON'T LEAVE ME BEHIND!

I WANT TO STAY WITH YOU TILL THE END!

YAAH!
WE MUST FIGHT! DON'T STAIN THE HONOR OF THE KNIGHTS OF HYRULE!
LISTEN UP!
GET IT DONE!
GO, LINK!
CAN I ENTRUST MIDNA TO YOU?

CHOK

GWOH
HWP

...BUT FOR NOW...
...LEND ME YOUR STRENGTH FOR THIS FIGHT!
YOU DON'T HAVE TO BELIEVE ME...
BUT DO IT AFTER WE DEFEAT THE DEMON KING!
IF SIDING WITH THE TWILIGHT REALM IS A SIN...
...YOU CAN BEAT, BANISH, OR EXECUTE ME!

...
EVEN YOU, ASHEI?
SNAP OUT OF IT!
TO HIDE YOUR OWN WEAKNESS AND SHAME...
...YOU'RE JUST LOOKING FOR AN EVIL YOU CAN SAFELY OPPOSE.
WHY DO YOU HATE THE TWILIGHT REALM SO MUCH?
I DON'T UNDER-STAND, AURU.
UNLESS YOU THINK WE CAN WIN THIS BATTLE ALONE?
WHY SHOULDN'T WE ALLY WITH THEM TO CONFRONT OUR MUTUAL ENEMY?
AURU! WE AREN'T FIGHTING THE TWILIGHT REALM!
THE TRUE ENEMY...
...INFESTS THE CASTLE!
THE DEMON KING GANONDORF!

THE PEOPLE OF TWILIGHT HELPED US!

THEY LIVED WITH US AND TOOK CARE OF US!
IT'S TRUE.
THANKS TO THEM, I DIDN'T WASTE AWAY TO NOTHING!

THEY'RE FRIENDS!
THEY MAY LOOK A LITTLE DIFFERENT, BUT THEY'RE PEOPLE JUST LIKE US!
THEY AREN'T MON-STERS!
WHEN MAYOR GRISNA ARRIVES, HE'LL CONFIRM IT, AND SO WILL ALL THE OTHER RESIDENTS!

GULP

THEY'RE MUCH MORE RELIABLE THAN SOLDIERS WHO FLEE IN THE FACE OF THE ENEMY.

I, FOR ONE, BELIEVE THOSE BOYS.
TMP

STOMP
WE'RE FROM THE CITY GUARDING THE DESERT BORDER!
LISTEN ...
WE WERE READY TO DIE!
HOW DO YOU THINK WE GOT BACK TO THIS WORLD ALIVE?
THE WHOLE CITY GOT FLIPPED INTO THE TWILIGHT REALM AND WE SPENT YEARS THERE WAITING FOR HELP.

WHUH?!
THE HERO OF HYRULE... TURNING HIS SWORD ON US?!
LINK! HAVE YOU LOST YOUR MIND?!
BUT...
WHY WOULD I?!
I DON'T WANT TO!
...NO MATTER WHO THEY ARE!
...MIDNA IS IMPORTANT TO ME.
I WON'T LET ANYONE HARM HER...

IF YOU'RE SIDING WITH THAT MONSTER, YOU'RE OUR ENEMY TOO!
LIGHT... OR SHADOW?!
WHOSE SIDE ARE YOU ON?

IF IT GOES WILD, WE'LL BE HELPLESS!
IT'LL KILL US TOO!
SHE HELPED US!
BUT WHAT WOULD HAVE HAPPENED TO US WITHOUT THAT POWER?!
THE POWER OF SHADOW IS DANGEROUS! IT CAN DESTROY THE WORLD OF LIGHT!
WE DON'T NEED IT!
THIS IS DIFFER-ENT!
PLEASE, LISTEN!
LINK! AS A DEFENDER OF HYRULE, YOU MUST DESTROY THE CREATURES OF SHADOW!

LINK...
...GET AWAY FROM THAT THING.

AURU?

GET AWAY!
IT'S DANGER-OUS!

D-DON'T MOVE!
IT'S CLEARLY A MONSTER!

SHE WON'T USE THE POWER OF SHADOW ANYMORE.
IT'S OKAY.
AURU ... WAIT.

I'M NOT STRONG ENOUGH. NOT GOOD ENOUGH...

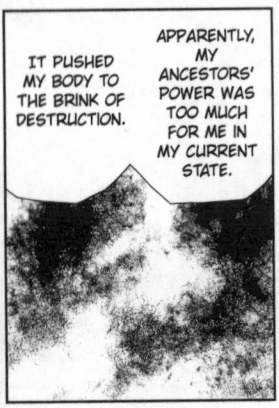
IT PUSHED MY BODY TO THE BRINK OF DESTRUCTION.
APPARENTLY, MY ANCESTORS' POWER WAS TOO MUCH FOR ME IN MY CURRENT STATE.

WHAT'S WRONG?
MIDNA?! HANG IN THERE!

LEAVE THE REST TO ME.

YOU DON'T HAVE TO FIGHT ANYMORE!
THAT'S ALL RIGHT. REST NOW.

MIDNA! ARE YOU ALL RIGHT?
I BETRAYED YOU.
...THE UNFOR-GIVABLE.
I'VE DONE...
... GOOD.
THAT'S ...
REALLY ...?
YOU JUST HAD A LITTLE TROUBLE CONTROLLING THE POWER.
HUSH NOW.
BUT THE BARRIER COVERING THE CASTLE IS GONE...
... THANKS TO YOU!

PW
A
H
UNGH!
WHUD
LINK! THANK THE GODS!

LINK!
RATTL
RATTL
RATTL
RATTL
RATTL

DEMON KING...
HEF
HEF
HEF
... I WILL KILL YOU!
HEF
HEF
DEMON KING...
M-MIDNA...
KRUK
D-DON'T!
KRCH
GRUK
GOOOO

HWOO
M...
MIDNA?!
HFF
HFF
HFF

RESCUE PRINCESS ZELDA AS QUICKLY AS YOU CAN!
GO, LINK! LEAVE THEM TO US!
HERE COME THE MONSTERS!
WHAH?!

TAKE THIS!
FWSH
GANONDORF IS IN THE THRONE ROOM OF THAT KEEP!

GRAAAA
KING
THUP
THUP

SLASH

#50. THE LORD'S HALL, PART 1
THE BARRIER'S GONE!
WAAA
CHAAARGE !!
KRRRR

FLASH

VN NN
TOM

BWOOO

WSH
WHOW
AAGH
WHP
EMB
EMB

THE SHADOW BEASTS!
GRR
RHA
WHAT THE...?
MONSTERS ATTACKING MON-STERS ?!
YOU GOT IT!
LET'S GO!

THWAP
KRKK
KOOM
KRAK

...COME TO MY SIDE...
...AND FIGHT!
HWOO

COME...
THRMM
MMM

HWOOSH
I AM THE LEADER OF THE TWILI.
SHADOW BEASTS LEFT BEHIND...
...IN THE WORLD OF LIGHT.
HEAR ME, MY PEOPLE:

...WHAT'S THAT?!
W... W...
IS THAT WHAT SHE BECOMES WHEN SHE RELEASES THE POWER OF SHADOW?!
MIDNA ?!
IT'S...
...A M-MONSTER.

GW

THRMMMM

WHAT HAPPENED ?!
MIDNA ...?
GWOOOOOO
?!

SKSHT
GYAH!
FWSSSH
TINK
OOF!
WHAM
BUSH
TWOOT

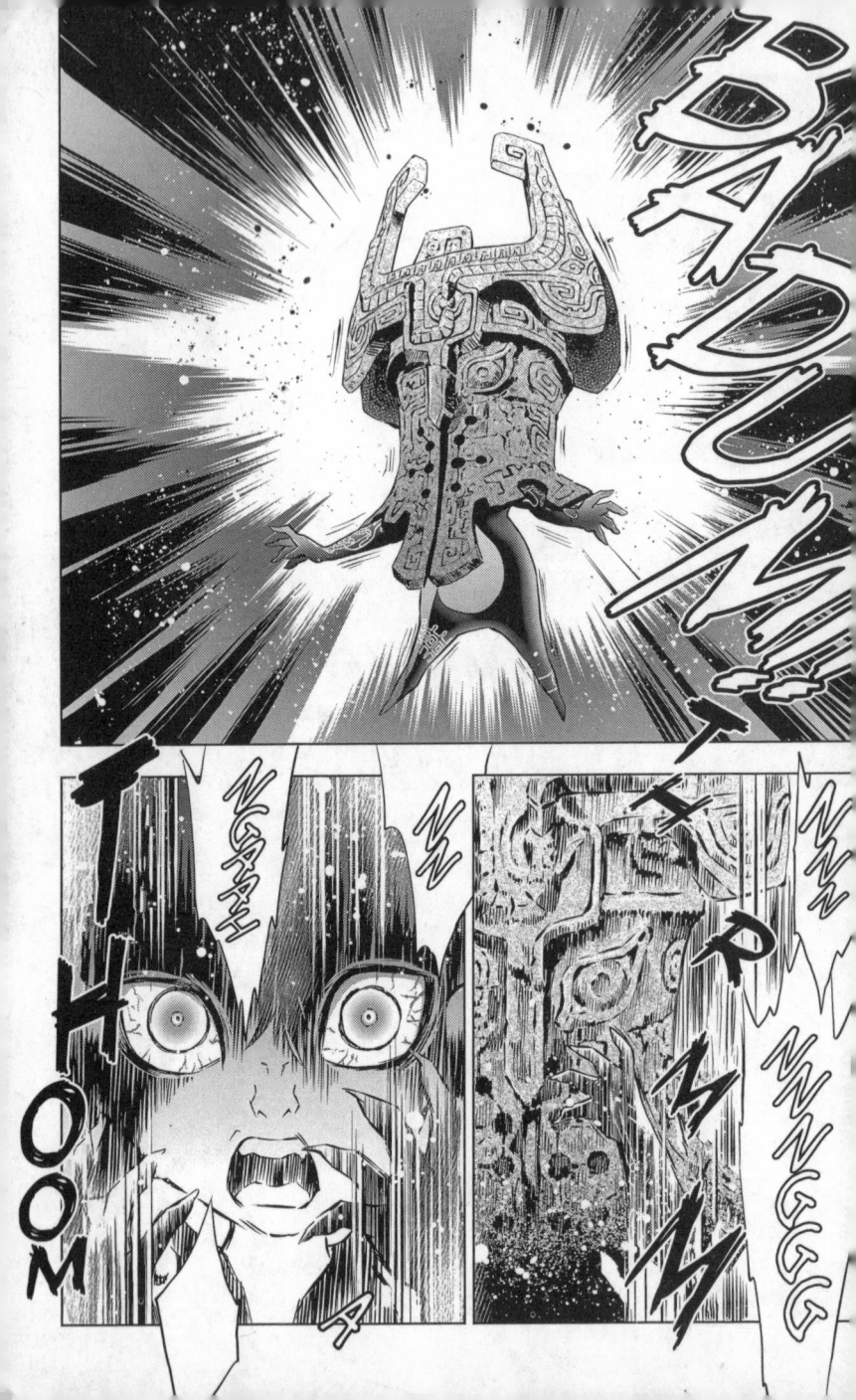
BADUMM
NNN
NNNGGG
NGAAH
THOOM

GRANT ME YOUR STRENGTH!
ZZK
ANCIENT MAGIC!
I'M BETTING...
...IT'LL HELP US DEFEAT THE KING OF DARKNESS.
THE STRENGTH ...
...TO DEFEAT THE DEMON KING!

I WONDER WHAT IT'S LIKE?
THE POWERFUL ANCIENT MAGIC THAT ZANT WAS OBSESSED WITH ACQUIRING...
...THIS IS PRECISELY THE TIME TO PUT THAT POWER TO USE.
BUT...
...
WHAT HAPPENS IF SOMEONE POSSESSES IT?
THEY SAY IT'S AN IMMENSE POWER THE GODS FORBADE AND SEALED AWAY.
NO ONE KNOWS.

WHAT A VILE BARRIER!
I WON'T LET YOU MONSTERS HAVE YOUR WAY ANY LONGER!
VOOM

AND YOU'RE HIS FRIENDS?
LINK'S VANISHED HOMETOWN RETURNED?!
WE'RE THANKFUL FOR ALL THE HELP WE CAN GET.
...IN THE CITY GUARDING THE BORDER.
I'M DARPA.
...
AND WE TRAINED TOGETHER...
WE'RE LINK'S FRIENDS ...
ZEU.
RIOMA.
QUIT YAPPING AND FOCUS OR THE MONSTERS WILL KILL YOU!
I'VE ALWAYS ADMIRED THEM, SO TO FIGHT ALONGSIDE YOU IS...
...LIKE...
... AN HONOR !
ARE ...
ARE YOU THE KNIGHTS OF HYRULE?!
I'M RUSL. PROUD TO FIGHT BY YOUR SIDE!
ALL RIGHT!
REINFORCEMENTS?
THAT'LL HELP!
OTHER WARRIORS FROM THE CITY ARE PREPARING TO JOIN US!
Y-Yeah.

YOU CAN DO THAT?
!
GOT IT!
I'LL BREACH THAT BARRIER...
...THEN YOU CAN TAKE THE BATTLE INSIDE!
WHO ARE YOU BOYS?
DEFEND WITH AN UMBRELLA FORMATION!
WE'LL COVER LINK'S FLANK!
You got it!
FOLLOW MIDNA!

SLA
SH
LINK!
WHERE DID YOU COME FROM?
WHERE HAVE YOU BEEN?!
THE RULER OF TWILIGHT, YOU SAY?!
THE POWER OF MIDNA, THE RULER OF TWILIGHT, BROUGHT US HERE.
IS SHE ON *OUR* SIDE?
OF COURSE!
SHE'S A TRUE FRIEND!
WE'VE COME FROM THE TWILIGHT REALM.

LOOKS LIKE GANONDORF HAS LAUNCHED AN ALL-OUT ATTACK!
WE GOT BACK JUST IN TIME FOR THE BIG FIGHT, HUH? THIS'LL TEST OUR METTLE!

IF HE WERE HERE, HE'D FIND A WAY!
WHAT WAS IT LINK SAID?
SHADOW MAGIC, EH?
HMPH!
LORD AURU, EVACUATE TO THE TAVERN!
ASHEI! LOOK OUT!

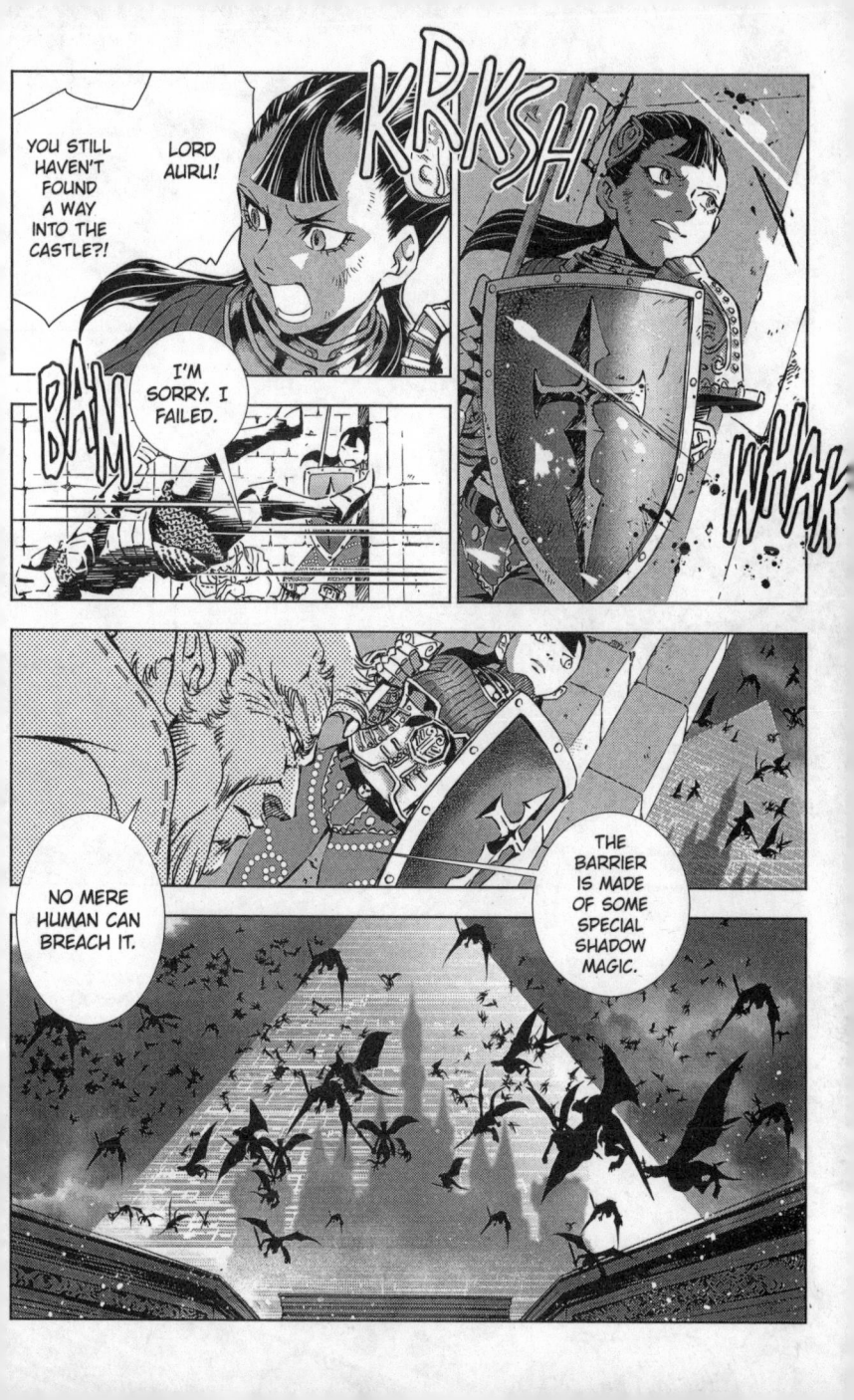
YOU STILL HAVEN'T FOUND A WAY INTO THE CASTLE?!
LORD AURU!
KRKSH
BAM
I'M SORRY. I FAILED.
WHAK
NO MERE HUMAN CAN BREACH IT.
THE BARRIER IS MADE OF SOME SPECIAL SHADOW MAGIC.

I BEAR THIS SWORD...
...SO I CAN PROTECT MY HOME IN TIMES LIKE THESE!
LINK... WHERE ARE YOU?!
IF ONLY YOU WERE HERE NOW!

THIS TIME IT MAY BE THE END.
RUSL! YOUR WIFE JUST HAD A BABY!
GO TO HER! HURRY HOME!
NO ONE WILL BLAME YOU.
YOU FOOL!
IF WE DON'T STOP THEM HERE, HOW CAN I PROTECT MY WIFE AND CHILD?!

FIGHT!
STAND YOUR GROUND!
DON'T RUN!

FIGHT TO SURVIVE!
IF YOU RUN THEN WE'RE DONE FOR!

WA AH

N-NO!
WE CAN'T WIN!

KK
IMP
IMP
IMP
GULP...
WAAAA

PAAAAA
A

GRAAAH
GYAA

THIS MOVE BY THE ENEMY IS AN OPPORTUNITY ...
...TO TAKE BACK THE CASTLE EVEN IF IT COSTS US OUR LIVES!
HERE WE GO!
AS LONG AS THERE ARE KNIGHTS OF HYRULE...
...WE WILL NOT GIVE IN TO MONSTERS!
LOOSE!
THWP
THWP
THWP
POOAR

STAND FIRM!

UMM... WOW WHOA
WHAT A HUGE ARMY!
OUR WORST FEARS ARE REALIZED!
THEY'RE NOT JUST ATTACKING CASTLE TOWN, BUT ALL OF HYRULE!

PRINCE RALIS!
THE RMY OF NSTERS SO VAST FILLS TH SKY ID SEA!
THE MONSTERS ARE UPON US!
ZORA WARRIORS! PREPARE YOURSELVES!
LINK!
FLUP
FLUP
FLUP
FLUP
RAAA

ACCEPT MY RULE!
FLDW
TMP
FDW

I WILL MERGE LIGHT AND SHADOW INTO MAGNIFICENT DARKNESS...
... AND COVER THE ENTIRE WORLD!
TMP
TMP

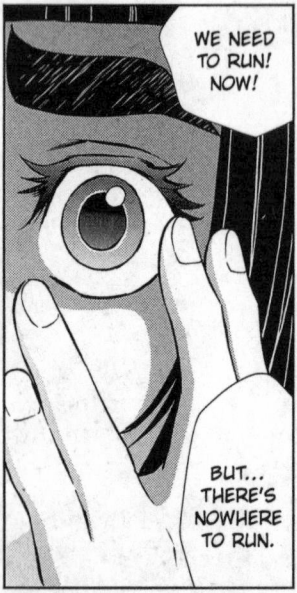
WE NEED TO RUN! NOW!
BUT... THERE'S NOWHERE TO RUN.

WHAT'S THAT BLACK CLOUD?
LUDA?

WHAT?!
THE DARKNESS WILL SWALLOW ...
...ALL LIFE IN HYRULE!

THIS TIME, WE REALLY ARE...
...ALL GOING TO DIE AND DISAPPEAR!

I'M READY! PREPARE TO WARP!
SHUSSH

GASP
IT'S A VAST ARMY OF MONSTERS!
GRAUK
GRAUK
THERE ISN'T A MOMENT TO LOSE!
IT'S FINALLY BEGINNING.
I'VE NEVER ENCOUNTERED HIM DIRECTLY.
WE'VE NEVER MET, BUT...
THE DEMON KING...
WHAT IS GANONDORF LIKE?
...SINCE BEFORE I WAS BORN...
...HE HAS BEEN THE ENEMY I'M DESTINED TO FIGHT!

WHAT'S HAPPENING AT HYRULE CASTLE?!
LINK...
TMP
TMP
TMP
TMP
HEY! LOOK AT THAT CLOUD!
WHAT ABOUT THE KNIGHTS OF HYRULE?
THE DEMON KING HAS SEIZED THE CASTLE?
ZANT HAS RAISED A BARRIER THAT KEEPS US FROM ENTERING.
THEY'RE BUSY PROTECTING THE PEOPLE OF CASTLE TOWN.
NO... WAIT! THAT'S NO CLOUD!
IT ALMOST SEEMS TO BE ALIVE!
IT'S DARK... AND CREEPY!

I WILL KILL THE HERO ONCE AND FOR ALL! HE WILL NEVER BE REBORN...
...AND HYRULE WILL FALL TO RUIN!
WITH THE FLAME OF MY HATRED ...
...I WILL STEAL EVERY-THING ...
...AND BURN IT ALL TO THE GROUND!

AT LAST...
THE TIME HAS COME! I WILL BE RID OF THIS CURSE!
I WILL SEVER THE HATEFUL CHAINS...
OF THIS TRIFORCE!

#49. THE POWER OF SHADOW

THE LEGEND OF ZELDA™

·Twilight Princess·

10

CONTENTS

*49. The Power of Shadow 3

*50. The Lord's Hall, Part 1 47

*51. The Lord's Hall, Part 2 80

*52. The Lord's Hall, Part 3 118

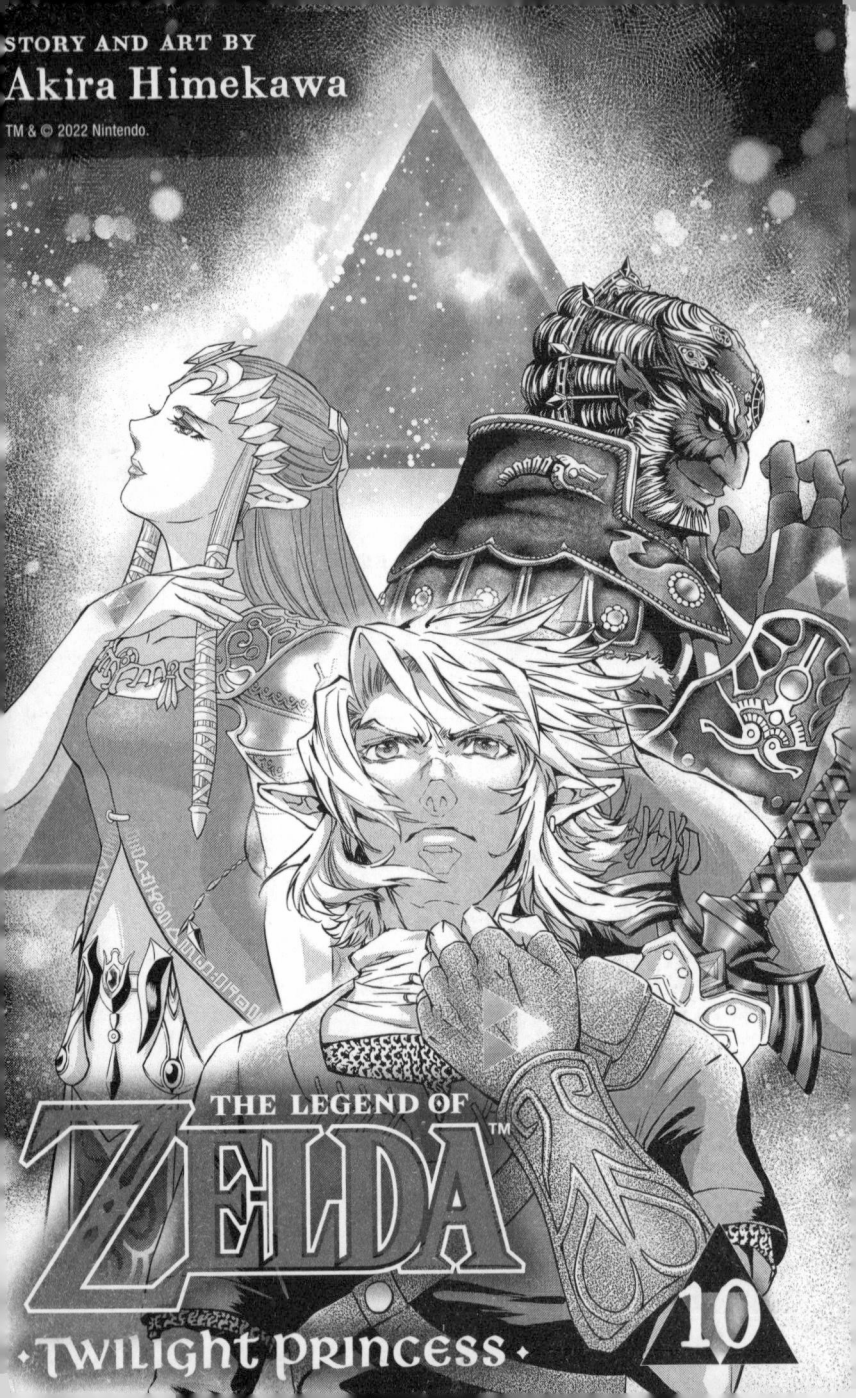
STORY AND ART BY
Akira Himekawa
TM & © 2022 Nintendo.
THE LEGEND OF
ZELDA
TWILIGHT PRINCESS
10